St. Edward, King and Martyr

Goscelin of Saint-Bertin
Translated by Ryan Grant

Introduction by Eric Sammons

Copyright © 2020 Saragossa Press
Published by Saragossa Press, Cincinnati, Ohio.
www.saragossapress.com
All rights reserved.

ISBN: 1-7347656-0-7
ISBN-13: 978-1-7347656-0-1

Front Cover Art: "The Wicked Queen Elfrida" by Joseph Martin Kronheim.
Back Cover Art: King Edward in an early fourteenth century *Genealogical Roll of the Kings of England*.

DEDICATION

To
St. Edward, King and Martyr.
Pray for us!

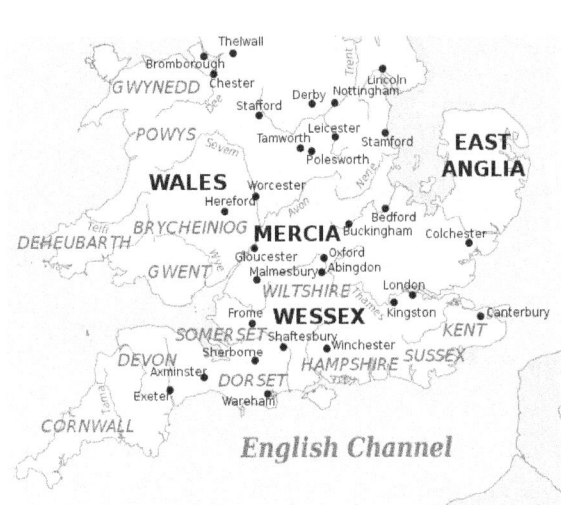

10th Century England and Wales

CONTENTS

Introduction 1
The Passion of St. Edward, King and Martyr 21

INTRODUCTION

The Passion of St. Edward, King and Martyr tells the story of a young king of England killed under scandalous circumstances in the 10th century. The protagonist, St. Edward the Martyr, is an obscure figure today, often confused with St. Edward the Confessor, a more well-known English King and Saint who lived and reigned a century later, or with St. Edmund the Martyr, a King of East Anglia who lived and reigned a century earlier and was England's original patron saint. Yet in the years following his death, devotion to St. Edward the Martyr was widespread in England, and many miracles were attributed to his intercession.

The Anglo-Saxon Period

St. Edward the Martyr lived and died in the latter days of the Anglo-Saxon period, which lasted from the end of Roman rule in AD 410 to the Norman

Invasion in AD 1066. The period gets its name from the large influx of Germanic tribes from the regions of Anglia and Saxony in Europe who immigrated to the island. During these six centuries, the area now known as England was transformed dramatically.

After the Roman Empire retreated to the continent after the sack of Rome in 410, England devolved into a chaotic and mostly pagan land ruled by many local chieftains. With the coming of St. Augustine of Canterbury in 597, England became more Christianized and more centralized, although the area remained carved into multiple kingdoms for centuries. Starting in the late 8th century, the Anglo-Saxons suffered through a century of Viking raids, causing substantial instability for most inhabitants. But in the second half of the ninth century, Alfred, King of Wessex (r. 871–899) succeeded in uniting the Anglo-Saxons and warding off the Vikings. This eventually led to the creation of the kingdom of England in 927 under Alfred's grandson, King Æthelstan (r. 927–939).

Along with bringing a semblance of stability to the land, Alfred also encouraged learning and Christianity. He saw it as a duty of the King to support the Church and advance her work, and this conception of kingship continued after his reign. Although the tenth century is now considered the darkest of the European "Dark Ages," this period was one of Christian progress in England. The great figure of the time was St. Dunstan, who was instrumental in building up monastic life. Dunstan, born c. 908, was a learned monk who was Abbot of Glastonbury Abbey, and eventually rose in rank to become the Archbishop of Canterbury. His influence over both the English Church as well as the nation at that time was vast.

As Abbot, Dunstan worked tirelessly to reform Glastonbury Abbey, using the Rule of St. Benedict as his basis. With the support of England's ruling family during the reign of King Eadred (r. 946–955), Dunstan extended his monastic reforms beyond Glastonbury. In Dunstan's time, it was common—yet unlawful—for married clergy to live in the monasteries. Dunstan saw the inclusion of these so-called "white clergy" as a barrier to a return to monastic principles and worked to end this practice. Although Dunstan at one point entered into a feud with King Eadred's successor, Eadwig (r. 955–959), and even had to flee the island for a brief time, he eventually returned to England

and to royal favor and was consecrated bishop of Worcester, and then a year later, of London.

King Edgar the Peaceful and St. Dunstan

King Eadwig died in 959 and was succeeded by Edgar, St. Edward's father. Known as "the Peaceful," Edgar ruled in a time particularly marked by Christian advancement and stability (as can be deduced from his moniker). Soon after Edgar gained the throne, Dunstan became the Archbishop of Canterbury, the most powerful cleric in England. He was, in essence, the Prime Minister of the kingdom, appointing bishops and pushing through many reforms of both the monasteries and the English Church. In 973, Dunstan officiated at the coronation of King Edgar. The coronation, occurring 14 years after Edgar's reign had begun, was seen as the culmination of his reign rather than its initiation. Interestingly, it is this regal coronation that still forms the basis of the modern-day British coronation ceremony.

At this point, the Church and the State, under Dunstan and Edgar respectively, jointly ruled England in relative harmony. In terms of stability and peace, this was the pinnacle of the Anglo-

Saxon period, although there were factions among the nobles who resented Dunstan's influence on the King.

The Contested Succession

When King Edgar died just two years later in 975, a dispute arose over his succession which brought those factions into the open. At this time rules of succession were not as clear-cut as they later became. Usually the eldest son was the successor, but other factors came into play, including whether the son was legitimately born, as well as the level of support for him among the leading families in the kingdom. As Edgar's eldest son, 13-year-old Edward had the strongest claim to the throne. However, Edward's mother was dead, and there was doubt regarding Edward's legitimacy… including rumors that Edward was the product of an illicit liaison between Edgar and a nun. Edgar's second son was seven-year-old Ethelred (Æthelred). Ethelred was the son of Edgar's wife, the ambitious Queen Elfrida (Ælfthryth), and thus his legitimacy was unquestioned.

St. Dunstan and the Church authorities supported Edward's claim to the throne, while the forces that sought diminishment of the Church's power and opposed monastic reform supported Elfrida's son, Ethelred. After a brief dispute, Dunstan's considerable influence won out. He crowned the young Edward as King of England.

King Edward's Reign

Even before ascending to the throne, Edward was known as a pious young man and was popular among the people. Once he became king, he was generous to the poor, promoted the Christian Faith, and supported Dunstan's monastic reforms.

Unfortunately, soon after Edward's accession, hopes that he would have a peaceful reign like his father Edgar were quickly dashed. Many prominent men, led by the nobleman Elfhere, coveted the lands controlled by the monasteries and attacked these Christian centers in order to endow themselves with more land and resources. The "white clergy"—those married clergymen who had been expelled from the monasteries previously—conspired to return to their old dwellings. At the same time, England was struck by a famine.

King Edward and Archbishop Dunstan held a series of contentious councils with the other leaders of the Church and the State, but they were unable to satisfy their enemies without compromising their Christian convictions. Through all the dissension and pressure, the young Edward maintained his support of Dunstan and the Church. And so, only three years into Edward's reign, his enemies decided to rid themselves of this troublesome king.

The Murder of a King

On the fateful day, the young king was hunting with some others near Wareham in Dorset. He was separated from his group and decided to ride over to the home of his brother Ethelred, at Corfe Castle, which lies on the southern coast of England. Hearing that Edward was nearing the castle, Ethelred's mother Elfrida took advantage of the situation to plot his murder.

As King Edward approached on horseback, Elfrida came out to greet him and handed him a chalice of wine. One of the queen's servants then approached the King and gave him a kiss of greeting to show that Edward was a welcome visitor. However, as Edward turned, the servant, as the *Passion* says, then "pierced his bowels with a dagger." Some accounts of Edward's death relate that Edward fell from his horse, but with one foot caught in a stirrup, his body was then dragged away by his horse. The

Passion simply says he fell to the ground, lifeless, and that "the beloved of God dying, substituted heavenly things for earthly things, and in place of a perishable and momentary crown, took up the imperishable crown of eternal happiness." It was the 18th of March, 978. (Although all agree on the day, some sources indicate 979, and the *Passion* says 981.)

The body of Edward was hidden in the home of a blind woman nearby. The next night she was cured of her blindness and gave credit to the recently-killed king. Elfrida heard of this miracle and, desiring to quell any potential veneration of her step-son, had the body moved and hidden in a marshy location. However, a year later the body was found when a pillar of fire miraculously appeared to let the faithful know where Edward lay. It was then moved to a humble tomb in a small nearby church.

The Cult of St. Edward

Veneration of Edward grew quickly after his death. The *Passion* was written about 100 years later, but already by then there was widespread and established devotion to the young martyr-king. Viking raids had resumed soon after Edward's death, and many saw them as divine punishment for the murder of the pious youth. The people proclaimed him a saint and a martyr. In 1008, only thirty years after his murder, Edward was officially canonized by an act of the All-English Council, presided over by the Archbishop of Canterbury, St. Alphege. The Council ordered that Edward's feast day be observed throughout England. Eleventh century liturgical calendars contain entries for Edward's feast, with many including the entry in capital letters, indicating a major feast.

Besides Edward's defense of the Church during his life, another reason for the rapid development of his cult was the multitude of miracles attributed to him after his death, many of which are related in the *Passion* account. In 981—three years after his death—Edward's relics were translated from Wareham to Shaftesbury with much pomp and celebration. At one point on the path of the procession, two men who were partially paralyzed lay near the route. The men carrying Edward's body on a bier lowered it down to the poor men. Immediately the men were healed of their paralysis and walked again.

For the next 20 years countless miracles were attributed to the martyr-king. While many occurred at Edward's tomb in Shaftesbury, people throughout England saw visions of the young king that led to healings of body and soul. Edward's brother King Ethelred proclaimed, "my brother Edward…covered in his own blood, the Lord himself has deigned to magnify by many signs of power."

In 1001, another miracle occurred that confirmed the martyr-king's sanctity. Up until this time Edward's casket was buried in the earth, but it began to rise up from the ground by its own power. A local monk had a vision in which Edward said to him, "Go to the convent called by the famous name of Shaftesbury and take commands to the nun Ethelfreda who is in charge of the other servants of God there. You will say to her that I do not wish to remain any longer in the place where I now lie, and command her on my behalf to report this to my brother without delay." The monk followed Edward's orders, and soon the Abbess Ethelfreda told the story to King Ethelred.

Edward's brother realized that this was a sign from God, who wanted the martyr-king's body to be given greater veneration. Thus, the King ordered that a new and glorious tomb be made for his brother's body. Further, as Edward's tomb was exhumed and opened, a beautiful fragrance came from it, confirming his sanctity to all those present. Edward's body was then carefully laid in the new tomb, and carried in procession to its new resting place. King Ethelred ordered that three different days be set aside as feast days for his brother: March 18, the anniversary of Edward's death and entry into heaven; February 13, the anniversary of his tomb's translation to Shaftesbury; and June 20, the anniversary of the placement of his body in the new tomb. Edward's fame became so great that the town of Shaftesbury where his tomb resided became known as "Edwardstowe" in his honor. It kept this name until the time of Henry VIII and the Reformation.

Miracles continued to occur at Edward's tomb, particularly healings which could only be attributed to heavenly intercession, such as the curing of leprosy and of blindness. Even more glorious, men and women deep in sin came to repentance through Edward's intercession.

No miracle, however, was greater than the one involving she who was responsible for Edward's death: his step-mother Queen Elfrida. In the years following Edward's death, Elfrida heard of the miracles surrounding him. Then, after learning of the two paralyzed men who were healed by contact with Edward's bier, Elfrida came to a realization of her crime. She wished to travel to Shaftesbury to ask forgiveness; however, on the way her horse stopped and would not go any further. Elfrida took this as a sign that it was her sins that held the horse back, and so continued the journey on foot in penance. But then she herself was held back by a mysterious force. She cried out to heaven begging forgiveness, and lived the rest of her life—almost 20 years—in a convent, doing penance for her terrible sin.

Diminishing Cult and Recovering the Relics

In spite of its auspicious beginnings, over time the cult of St. Edward Martyr began to diminish. One reason might be that, after the Norman Invasion in 1066 and the establishment of the House of Normandy on the English throne, the new ruling family had little desire to promote the royal House of Wessex to which Edward belonged. Then, during the dissolution of the monasteries under

INTRODUCTION

King Henry VIII in the 16th century, Shaftesbury Abbey, where Edward's tomb still resided, was destroyed. Fortunately the faithful saved the Saint's relics from desecration by hiding them elsewhere in the monastery grounds.

The story of St. Edward the Martyr might have ended there but for another miracle four centuries later. In the early 1930's, amateur archeologist J. Wilson-Claridge uncovered some well-preserved bones under the ruins of Shaftesbury Abbey. A thorough examination was performed by Dr. T.E.A. Stowell. He determined that the bones were those of a young man, a Saxon, and that certain of the bones were injured in a manner consistent with a person being dragged over the pommel of a saddle and having a leg twisted in a stirrup. He concluded his report, "I cannot escape the conviction, on historical, anatomical and surgical grounds that beyond reasonable doubt, we have here the bones of St. Edward, King and Martyr."[1]

A legal battle ensued over possession of the relics. Mr. Wilson-Claridge wanted to donate the relics to

---

[1] Wilson-Claridge, J, *The Recorded Miracles of St. Edward the Martyr*, (Brookwood: King Edward Orthodox Trust Company, 1984), p. 10.

the Russian Orthodox Church Outside Russia, believing that ROCOR would best preserve and properly venerate the holy relics. The town of Shaftesbury, however, argued that the relics should be in its possession. At one point the Attorney General decided that they rightly belonged to the Queen of England. Eventually, however, Mr. Wilson-Claridge's wishes were honored, and the relics were given to the Orthodox Church of St. Edward the Martyr in Brookwood Cemetery near Woking in Surrey, England, and it is there that they currently reside.

Modern Cult

The story of St. Edward the Martyr does not end there, however. After the recovery of his relics, miracles again began to be attributed to his heavenly intercession. They became so numerous that J. Wilson-Claridge, the man who rediscovered Edward's relics, collected many of them into a booklet.

One miracle in particular will be recounted here.[2] An English Orthodox Christian found herself

---

[2] This story can be found at
https://www.orthodox.net/western-saints/edward.html
(retrieved on 3/11/2020).

pregnant. She was overjoyed, but soon learned that she had contracted toxoplasmosis, and the baby would be born with no legs and no arms. Her doctors advised her to abort her child, but due to her Christian faith, she refused.

Later in the pregnancy she was told that the baby, a boy, would have arms and legs, but would be blind. At this time the mother was reading Mr. Wilson-Claridge's book on the miracles of St. Edward the Martyr, and she knew that Edward's first miracle was the healing of the blind woman. She decided to name the baby Edward in the saint's honor, and prayed to him for her unborn son.

Baby Edward was soon born, completely healthy and with normal eyesight. Yet the doctors noticed at his birth that the top half of the umbilical cord was completely blackened by infection, yet the discoloration miraculously stopped midway down the cord. The mother attributed this to the intercession of her son's namesake.

St. Edward the Martyr lived in a time before the Protestant Reformation and before the Great Schism, and as such, is venerated as a Saint by the Roman Catholic, Eastern Orthodox, and Anglican communions. Among Orthodox believers in Russia, Edward is perhaps the best known and most beloved English Saint today, and is known as "the Holy and Right-Believing King Edward the Martyr" and as a "passion-bearer." Further, along with the Orthodox parish in Surrey, many Catholic and Anglican parishes in England are dedicated to St. Edward the Martyr. The local Anglican parish in the village of Corfe Castle, where the Saint died, is appropriately dedicated to him. In the town of Shaftesbury, which held Edward's relics for so long, is the Roman Catholic parish of the Most Holy Name and St. Edward the Martyr. While St. Edward the Martyr may seem obscure today, his memory is still honored in those areas most closely associated with him, and by those who venerate him as a follower of Christ and a martyr for his Lord.

The Document

The Latin work *Passio Sancti Eadwardi Regis et Martyris* was written some time in the late 11th century, about 100 years after Edward's death. The term "passion" refers to the suffering and death of Jesus Christ, or of a saint who is killed for his faith in Christ. By naming this account *The Passion of St. Edward, King and Martyr*, the author is indicating that the king was killed for his Christian beliefs and that he met death in a Christ-like manner.

There is some debate as to the identity of the author, but in most likelihood it was written by Goscelin of Saint-Bertin (c. 1035–c. 1100), a Benedictine monk who wrote many hagiographies, including one on St. Edward's sister, St. Edith. It was composed during the 1070's, when Goscelin was writing other hagiographies of saints of Western England. After that time, he moved to Canterbury and focused on Canterbury saints.

The *Passion* is the fruition of the developing cult of St. Edward. Before the *Passion* was written, Edward's martyrdom had already been mentioned in the *Anglo-Saxon Chronicle*, and as we have seen, feast days in his honor had been established for decades. Goscelin was known to travel to the locations where the events he was writing about occurred; as he compiled his accounts he used both written and oral testimonies. It appears that the traditions of Shaftesbury were a likely source for the *Passion*.

At least nine manuscripts of the *Passion* exist today, with slight variations among them. The Latin text used for this translation was compiled by Christine Fell (University of Leeds) in 1971 based upon her analysis of the various manuscripts. To my knowledge, this translation of the *Passion of St. Edward, King and Martyr* is the first complete translation into the English language.

Eric Sammons
March 18, 2020
Feast of St. Edward the Martyr

Icon of St. Edward the Martyr

The Passion of St. Edward, King and Martyr

The famous King Edward was descended from a high and most noble race of ancient kings. Since from the flower of his youth he was greater than these, after he was baptized by St. Dunstan, the archbishop of Canterbury, he began to be strong in integrity of morals.

King Edgar's Glorious Reign[1]

He appeared during the reign of a king of pious memory, Edgar by name, his father, who among all

---

[1] Subheadings are not in the original text and have been added to aid the reader.

the kings of Britain, was as prepared for wars as he was for the things of God, just as the morning star shines forth in the rays of uprightness. For, after he had prudently obtained the rule of the kingdom, with God's favor, he increased his kingdom with all the islands of the whole region that were previously ruled by different kings. Then, at the urging and teaching of the aforesaid Archbishop, and St. Æthelwold the Bishop of Winchester,[2] he saw to it that many destitute and empty monasteries in the country were restored at his own expense, while some were built from the ground up. He directed the abbots with a multitude of monks, that were going to live regularly in some of them, to be under the yoke of discipline. In some, however, he established congregations of consecrated women. So, after he arranged the affairs of the Church in this way, the glorious king was eager to become a bulwark of Holy Mother Church on the outside, and on the inside her trappings. Among the rest of the marks of his uprightness he decreed this, that he himself, as a provident pastor, would have care of those monks placed in the congregation, by

---

[2] Æthelwold of Winchester (904/9–984) was Bishop of Winchester from 963 to 984. He had been a monk at Glastonbury Abbey with St. Dunstan and, like Dunstan, was an instrumental reformer of the English monasteries.

frequently visiting and consoling them. His wife also, attended to the convents of consecrated nuns just as a most pious mother, so clearly a man would more suitably come to the assistance of men and a woman to women without any suspicion.

The same outstanding King Edgar also had another son from another wife by the name of Elfrida,[3] whose name was Ethelred.[4] Now the son we already mentioned, the youth Edward, was of good character, and his mind in no way exerted itself toward lascivious or enticing desires of the flesh; rather, he was zealous to show himself of such quality in all things, that he would please God above all in uprightness of mind and body, and to be loved by men with pious affection. Now, his father, seeing such a noble character flourishing in his most beloved son, rejoiced over his prudence and industry, hence he preordained and established by paternal custom that he must be enthroned in the royal throne by hereditary right after himself. Meanwhile, after composing and compelling, as we prefaced, the parts of the whole realm in peace and tranquility, Edgar was taken from this life by the Lord, as we believe, to gain eternal joys, in the year

---

[3] A traditional spelling of her name is Ælfthryth.
[4] A traditional spelling of his name is Æthelred.

of the Lord's incarnation 977,[5] the sixteenth year of his rule, in the month of July, on the eighth day of the same month.

King Edward Begins His Reign

After he died, his older son Edward, by the will of his father, as we have already reviewed, was chosen to take up the government of the realm by St. Dunstan and certain princes. But during the time of his consecration, when certain nobles of the country wanted to resist, St. Dunstan, persevering harmoniously in his election, took hold of the standard of the holy cross, which he customarily carried with him, placed it in the midst, and with the rest of the pious bishops, consecrated him as king, whom he also loved with all the paternal affection that he had, because he had taken him to himself like a son since he was a child.

Now, St. Edward was lifted up into the throne of the kingdom, he was directed by the Lord, the king of kings, in every path of justice and truth, and by whose help his days increased, relying upon Him with great disposition of soul and with supreme humility. For, in the newly acquired honor he soon accumulated these increases of his virtues of his

---

[5] King Edgar died in AD 975, not 977.

The anointing of Edward the Martyr at his coronation by St. Dunstan at Kingston-on-Thames, 975.
Illustration for the Illustrated London News Coronation Ceremony Record Number, 1902.

pristine goodness. Namely he delayed the counsels of youth and not of the wise, being advised by the aforesaid Archbishop to wholesomely focus his mind, and according to his counsel, as well as that of other religious and noteworthy men, he exercised his judgments in all things. As an imitator of his fathers' traditions, being effected very brave as much in military prowess as much as he was devoutly and strenuously focused in disposing ecclesiastical matters, he used a certain cruelty against enemies and those acting badly. But those living piously and especially constituted in sacred orders, he protected from every disturbance with adroit care, just as he learned from his most pious father. Besides, he also performed a certain rite of daily custom, feeding the hungry, restoring the poor, bestowing garments upon the naked, reckoning these things as a great profit, which he spent in such work. Then, among the people of the Angles everywhere a great joyfulness emerged, a great constancy of peace, great opulence of material goods. How much their king was provided with such things while still in the flower of youth, was affable in all things, praiseworthy in charity, decorous and joyful in face, esteemed in counsel and prudence!

Elfrida's Plot Against Edward

But the enemy of all good, the devil, hating those who lead happy lives and eager to disturb the common joy of the whole realm, incited Edward's mother-in-law,[8] Elfrida, with hatred for him. Her presumptuous shrewdness, which is so execrable in a woman, can be sufficiently adverted to from how the events transpired. For, after the fervor of hatred was enkindled, she began to think in what way the man of God could be uprooted from the realm, so that her own son Ethelred would be substituted in the kingdom without opposition. Therefore, such things as these were turning about in her mind for a while. When she opened the secrets of her heart with certain leading counselors, she made plans on this matter with them, asking and imploring that they would offer assent to her as one, and to devise in what order it could be carried out. Right away, all of them consented to his death, and felt that the sooner they carried out this deceitful treason the better.

As we said above, after the venerable man was confirmed in the kingdom he had then been in possession of the hereditary scepter for three years and eight months, as luck would have it he went out

---

[8] Elfrida was Edward's step-mother.

on a certain day with dogs and knights to hunt, near some village which is called Werham,[9] then it was held exceedingly great, but now it is a thin thicket, and since the site has been neglected, trees are discerned there to be covering up the field. Once the business had begun, he insisted on considerable travel. Then, calling to mind his adolescent brother Ethelred, he purposed to go visit him, because he loved him with a pure and upright heart.

Near the same forest there was a house of his mother-in-law in which the aforesaid boy was raised. This was in the place which came to be called Corph[10] by the inhabitants, and said to be three miles away from the village, where now a famous fortress has been constructed. At that place, although he had taken with him a small company when he set out, behold! After the fashion of men at play they wandered and were dispersed here and there, and Edward remained without any companion. But he, as he was alone at that house, since he looked at it from a spear's throw, aimed for it like a meek lamb, neither fearing nor dreading anyone, as he did not recollect anyone that he offended.

---

[9] Wareham.
[10] Corfe Castle.

The Murder of a King

While he approached it, her ministers announced to the most impious queen that King Edward was arriving there. She, being filled with wicked thought and treachery, and to gain fulfillment of the desires of her wickedness, rejoiced that at last it was the suitable time! She soon proceeded, hostile and with the courtiers of her iniquity, as if they were rejoicing in his arrival; they greeted him amicably and with charm, and invited him to stay as a guest. He declined, but gave notice that he wanted to see and address his brother. Changing to other schemes, she bid drink to be made ready for him without delay, namely while awaiting in secret, so that while he would incautiously taste the drink, a more opportune moment would provide itself to carry out what she had devised. Meanwhile, one who was even more bold in mind and more savage in wickedness, while feigning goodwill in imitation of the deed of Judas, the betrayer of the Lord, offered him a kiss of peace, so that while removing all suspicion and showing a deep love for him he might more easily strangle him. That also came to pass. For after taking the drink from the cupbearer he touched as far as the highest part of his mouth, and he that conferred the kiss to him, throwing

"Edward the Martyr" in
A Chronicle of England: B.C. 55 – A.D. 1485
by James William Edmund Doyle

himself behind him pierced his bowels with a dagger.

Being inflicted with a serious wound, while he turned little by little from there, he right away fell from the horse upon which he sat to the ground, lifeless. And so, the beloved of God dying, substituted heavenly things for earthly things, and in place of a perishable and momentary crown, took up the imperishable crown of eternal happiness.

This took place in the 981st year[11] of the Incarnate Word, and though it is impious to say, during the season of Lent, namely on the fifteenth day before the Kalends of April.[12] Yet, as we believe, so as to heap up the merits of its soldier, the divine dispensation so preordained it, that one who, by wearing down his flesh in annual Lenten fasting and by adhering to other good works according to the praiseworthy rite of Christians, he had prepared himself for the coming day of the Lord's resurrection, he was crowned with a good end, since in the very fruit of good works he was taken up into heavenly care by Christ; because according

---

[11] Likely 978 (or possibly 979).
[12] March 18.

to the sentence of the judge of all, everyone will be judged in the end in which he will have been found.

The Cover-Up of a Crime

Now, the aforesaid Elfrida hearing that he fell from his horse, not yet satisfying the frenzy of her wickedness, commanded Edward's body to be taken as soon as possible and it was thrown away in a certain home that was nearby, lest what had been done should become known. By whose command immediately the authors of the wicked crime ran up, dragged the body away by the feet in a beastly fashion, and contemptibly, as she had commanded, covered the body that had been thrown in the house with vile straw.

Moreover, there was in that little house a certain woman, blind from birth, whom the queen was customarily mindful of feeding as an alms. On the following night, while she spent the night there alone with the body, behold, it was an unseasonably stormy night and the glory of the Lord appearing in the same house, filled it with an immense splendor. Wherefore, the aforesaid poor woman, stricken with not a small amount of terror, since she prayed more attentively to the mercy of almighty God, merited to receive the long desired light,[13] bestowed by heavenly grace, from the merits of the man of God. In that place, on account of the memory of this event, a church was built by the faithful in testimony of the miracle, which endured even to our times.

Finding a Proper Burial Place

Meanwhile, when the first light of morning broke the darkness, while the queen learned what had happened from that feeble woman, and that a woman whom she knew was blind from birth was now able to see, she was disturbed in countenance and was changed into a different mind, fearing her execrable work could be manifested if she did not more attentively get rid of the body of the man of God. So, she commanded her courtiers to carry it off quickly, and put it in hidden and marshy places where she thought the country was less covered, lest it could be found by anyone else. After fulfilling her commands without delay, an edict was proclaimed in which she proposed nothing harsher than that nobody should weep over his ruin or altogether speak of it, thinking she could altogether blot his memory from the earth. After these things were so carried out, she immediately removed

---

[13] Sight.

herself to a certain great house that was hers by right, about ten miles distant from the aforesaid place which is called Bere,[14] that by so concealing what she had done in this matter no man would suspect her.

Meanwhile, her son Ethelred was so stricken with sorrow over the cruel death of his brother, that no one could console him, nor could he control his mourning or his tears. Wherefore, his mother, enkindled in her fury, violently beat him with candles, because she had nothing else at hand, so much so that he restrained his weeping. Henceforth, it is related for his whole life that he so hated candles that he scarcely permitted them to ever be lit in his presence.

Therefore, after these things, it transpired in the next year, when by heavenly piety his deserving martyr Edward was made known to the world, and it pleased him to declare how much merit he had with Him, He deigned to reveal his venerable body to certain faithful devoutly seeking it, and showed it with a heavenly proof. For around the place where his body was concealed, a pillar resembling fire appeared to be sent out above it, which seemed

---

[14] Bere Regis.

to frequently beam forth with the rays of its light all around it. Certain devout men from the nearby villa of Werham seeing it, gathered together and took it from the aforementioned place, and carried it into their villa. Then a vast gathering took place and the weeping of all carrying out the royal funeral rites, wailing in one voice, "Alas, what solace will we be able to hope for now, after these things? Who will free us from the attack of enemies now that the sweetest shepherd has been struck? Our joys have perished, nay more, the treaties of peace and concord of our nation have gone to ruin." Then, with the voices of these mourners the venerable body was brought to the Church of the Holy Mother of God, Mary. They most dutifully buried [him] at its eastern curtain, on the day of the ides of the month of February,[15] where a little wooden Church, which was later built by monks, and may be noticed even today. Also, a fountain in the place in which he had first lain, is discerned to flow sweet and clear water, from that time even to the present, and it is called the fountain of St. Edward, taken from the name of the holy man, where many benefits are daily conferred upon the sick, to the praise of Our Lord Jesus Christ.

---

[15] February 13.

The Translation to Shaftesbury

Meanwhile, rumor spread through the whole country of the Angles, the fraud and treachery of the queen was manifested, the celebration of the innocent king was extolled, the marks of his virtues and merits were preached everywhere. Therefore, a certain magnificent count, Aelfere by name, hearing the holy body was found by such an outstanding sign, was flooded with immense joy, and desiring to show fealty to his lord as though he were still living, decreed it should be translated[16] to a more worthy place. For the same man was famous, and having great compassion in regard to his cruel fall, he took it badly that such a precious pearl was hidden in so vile a place. To carry out such a worthy work, he invited bishops, and abbots with the nobles of the realm whom he could have, and he pleaded with them that they might agree with him and assist him in this business. He also sent an announcement to the abbess Wilfrida in a monastery which is called Wiltonia, and to summon [her] to carry out the exequies of such a man with the virgins consigned to her as appropriate.

---

[16] Moved. "Translated" is the term often used when sacred relics are moved from one location to another.

Moreover, in the same monastery there was a certain venerable virgin, the sister of the saint himself, great in life and influential by the integrity of her morals, called Edith,[17] who was the daughter of the aforementioned most glorious king Edgar and the same Wilfrida, not yet consecrated to God. Soon those coming together with supreme care and veneration, bishops also with abbots, as we said, were gathered together; the aforesaid Aelfere from Dorsata and not a few men and women joined the multitude, and arrived at Werham, where the body of the man of God had been handed over for burial, with great devotion. Now, right away, in the sight of all the people the body was found and removed from the earth, it was found unharmed in such a way that it was without any corruption, as if it had been buried on the same day. Moreover, the bishops and the other men of rank seeing this, with hymns and praises they glorified the mercy of almighty God, who deigned to show the innocence of his meritorious martyr with such a sign. But the aforesaid virgin, his own sister, running up, embraced that long-desired body, and while cherishing the holy hands, conferred many kisses. She watered the face with bountiful moistening of

---

[17] Saint Edith of Wilton (c. 963–c. 986) was a nun and a daughter of King Edgar.

tears, and could not satisfy her mind either with sighs or spiritual joy from so great a glory that her brother enjoyed. Then, it was taken up and placed on a bier by the hands of venerable men, and with great solemnity of clergy and people was taken down to Scepthonia,[18] because the same monastery was dedicated in honor of the holy Mother of God, Mary and was famous.

It was most appropriately built by that magnificent king, Alfred[19] of divine memory, who was the grandfather[20] of the holy man himself. The occasion of its building was that the same king having a daughter, Ailevam by name, and desiring to betroth her to the heavenly spouse, gave her to monastic discipline in the same Church, for love of which he frequently ennobled it with bountiful gifts. For among the characteristic relics of his gifts, a hundred hides[21] of land so restful and free, as he felt they would be better possessed forever, he made a gift of them to the monastery, of which,

---

[18] Shaftesbury.
[19] Alfred was King of Wessex 871–891.
[20] Alfred was Edward's great-great-grandfather.
[21] A "hide" (*hida*) means a parcel of land sufficient for a family. The actual acreage varies in official documents, and is uncertain for this period.

even today, the virgins serving Christ in them experience benefits.

Meanwhile, since on every side the multitude of each sex flocked to so unusual a thing from different parts, also two poor men, who had contracted an illness so bitter that they could hardly crawl on their hands and knees, arrived among the rest, meaning to implore the Lord and St. Edward on behalf of their misfortune. When they approached the bier, those who carried the sacred body above them laid it down to recover their health. Then right away, in the sight of the people, the poor men were restored to health. Such a thing being seen, the clamor of the people was lifted on high, and all venerated the merits of St. Edward in common.

The Repentance of Elfrida

The aforementioned queen, hearing in the meantime of the wonderful things done by the holy man, grew remorseful for the things which she had done. Next, after mounting her horse, she determined to go after him to ask forgiveness for her crime. This was hardly conceded to her while resisting divine force; for while she rode on the journey with her courtiers, behold she was so detained by a certain marvelous and unfathomable impediment, that the horse upon which she sat preferred rather more to go back than on the other hand to go ahead. Wishing to restrain it with the bridle, while turning this way, now that way, she could not advance with threats or kicks, and adverted that she was so detained by her sins. Wherefore, on the spot jumping from the horse to the ground, as on account of greater reverence she prepared to go on foot, but nevertheless, which is wonderful to relate, turning aside she availed to obtain what she desired, namely that she would openly make it known, that these things happened to her because of the crime that she had carried out against the man of God.

Meanwhile, the venerable body being lead to the aforementioned monastery, and being received suitably and in a praiseworthy fashion by the virgins serving God in it, it was buried in the north part of the principal altar with great honor on the twelfth day before the kalends of March,[22] where after these things many benefits were bestowed upon the infirm through him.

---

[22] February 18.

The Flood of Miracles

A certain matron, abiding in the remote parts of England, was weighed down by excessive weakness. Daily poured forth prayers for her health in the sight of the pious workman of God, on a certain night St. Edward stood next to her in a vision, and it is told he said things to her such as these. "When you rise in the morning, go to the place where I was given to be buried, and do not delay, because there you will receive a new and necessary shoe for your weakness." It was the case, as we can gather from a conjecture, that she had a serious flatness in her feet, and therefore, through new shoes the health of her feet was appointed. Waking, however, in the morning, when she related the dream that she had seen to a certain neighbor of hers, since she did not believe the vision, she asserted it was a phantom. Then, when the matron failed to heed the warnings of the aforesaid saint, the holy man again said to her in a vision, "Why spurning my commands, do you so neglect your healing? Go to my tomb and there you will be freed." After coming to her senses she said to him, "And who are you, Lord? Or where shall I find your tomb?" He answered, "I am king Edward, recently slain in an unjust killing, and I am buried in the Church of the Blessed Mary, Mother of God, in

Scephtonia." The woman however, waking in the morning, and thinking over what she had seen, soon took what was necessary for a journey, and made for the aforesaid monastery; arriving there, at length, when she entreated God and St. Edward with a humble heart, she was restored to health.

Besides, a great many miracles were frequently obtained at the tomb of the man of God, which due to the negligence of writers have not been committed to memory through writing. But we have preferred to leave unsaid what concerning the holy man other things which we have found faithfully written or which we learned from the relation of the faithful, lest we would speak thoughtlessly. Wherefore, after omitting these, we will open with a few words how his most holy relics have been lifted from the ground. Therefore, since already the merits of the glorious martyr Edward, by the wonderfulness of the miracles which were being done at his tomb daily, were declared far and wide, and for the heavenly dispensation, it pleased Him that his sacred relics be lifted from the ground, the saint himself began to manifest this with certain signs, and it should be done in such an order to show it with certain visions. For the tomb in which he rested was lifted from the earth with such ease, that it appeared clearly to all that he wished to be transferred from there.

Besides, he appeared to a certain religious man in a vision, to whom he said, "Go to the monastery which is called by a famous name Scephtonia, and to the virgin Aethelfreda who is there in charge of the others serving God, and give these commands. You will say, therefore, to her that in the place in which I now have lain for a long time I no longer wish to be, and that she will tell my brother without any delay to command it for my part." Who, rising in the morning, and thinking about the divine vision which he had received, went swiftly to the abbess as he had been commanded, and related to her all the things which had been shown to him in order. But she, giving thanks to almighty God for this, at once opened all to the ears of king Ethelred, and even made known the elevation of his tomb with supreme devotion. The king, hearing such glory of his brother, was filled with immense joy, and gladly, if he were given the opportunity, agreed to such a message, willingly desired to be present at its elevation. But surrounded with various and serious invasions of enemies on every side, could hardly be present for it. He directed messengers to the most reverend Wilsinus, bishop of Salisbury, and to a certain prelate of great sanctity, Elfsinus by name, and other men of venerable life, advising and commanding that they would repose the body of his brother elevated from the ground, in a worthy place. Those men, following the royal command at the aforesaid monastery with an innumerable crowd of men and women coming together in joyful spirit, opened the tomb with supreme veneration. Such a fragrant odor emanated from it that all who were present thought they had been constituted in the delights of Paradise; wherefore, even in such a place the whole Church was filled, that it appeared after the manner of a bright cloud. Then, the most glorious bishops devoutly approaching, took up the sacred relics from the tomb, and placing them in a casket lovingly prepared, they interred them in the holy of holies with the other relics of the saints in a spiritual ritual of divine exultation. The most holy body was elevated, therefore, in the twenty-first year after it had been buried, which was in the year 1001 of the Incarnation of the Lord, while the same Lord Jesus Christ was reigning, who with the Father and the Holy Spirit, lives and is glorified as God, for all ages of ages. Amen.

THE PASSION IS SET FORTH.

NOW BEGINS THE OCCURRENCE OF MIRACLES THAT WERE OBTAINED BY THE SAME.

A great many miracles were obtained through St. Edward, on which we have taken care to insert a few into this our little work. Therefore, in the times of the most glorious king Edward,[23] who was the son of aforementioned king Ethelred, namely the grandson[24] of St. Edward, there was a certain man abiding in parts beyond the sea, in the county of Virmandois,[25] John by name, who had contracted a serious anguish throughout his body. It was so bad, that was so closely related to his kidneys, he could not raise himself to any service of his members. This man, therefore, was admonished in a dream, that proceeding into England, he should head to the monastery of Scephtonia, in which St. Edward rested, because there he will receive healing. While he related this to his neighbors and relations, with their counsel and help, passing the straights of the sea, he arrived at the aforementioned monastery. At

---

[23] St. Edward the Confessor, King of England 1042–1066.
[24] St. Edward the Confessor was the nephew of St. Edward the Martyr.
[25] Vermandois; modern-day Picardy region of northern France.

length after different byways of places, [he arrived there]. While he prayed for some time to God and St. Edward for the return to safety and health, he was healed. Who also remained in the same monastery later serving even to the end of his life, on which nearly all remaining there who had seen him bore witness even to this day.

Not long after, a certain leper coming to the memory of the same saint, when in prayers and vigils for his illness he invoked divine help, he was cleansed from all the filth of leprosy.

Another miracle also happened through the same venerable man a little space of time after these, which we learned from the relation of respectable persons who saw it. For when the venerable man, Heremann, the bishop of the Church of Salisbury, in a certain time of his episcopate wandered to the parishes from pious curiosity, he took a shortcut for the sake of visiting the monastery of Scephtonia. A certain poor man whom he was accustomed to feed with his alms arrived in his company, for this was the pious custom of the same glorious bishop, and everywhere by a daily habit he picked up a journey, always having with him several weak and sick men that were lead to be refreshed by his nourishment. Now, while he delayed at the aforesaid monastery for a little while, the aforementioned blind man, at the lead of a servant who directed his steps, entered the Church meaning to pray. Where, while devoutly imploring the piety of almighty God for his illness, he prolonged the course of prayer even to vespers. The guards, keeping attentive care in the Church, finding him given to prayer, begged him to go out, but he would by no means go out, nay more he constantly professed that he awaited the mercy of God and St. Edward. When they heard this, they admired the faith of the man, and permitted him to lie in prayer, but his servant they compelled to go to his guesthouse. Meanwhile, while he rested for a while in that place, first he was filled with a great chill, then he was seized with an immense heat in his whole body, and then he received light. In the morning, when the fact was made known to certain men that he was in a healthier state, they could not easily be persuaded to believe him until they who already knew him were asked under the testimony of truth, and they affirmed that he had been blind for a long time. Then, at the command of the bishop, the virgins present in the Church serving God, gathered with a concourse of the people, breaking out in hymns and praises performed the proclamation of praises to Christ, who deigned to work these things by the merits of St. Edward.

In the same way, a certain man was brought in to the same Church, who was chained by heavy bonds on account of the sins that he had committed. The more he was constrained with bitter sorrow, the more devoted he was, and he poured forth prayers in the sight of the majesty of God, so by the merits of the man of God, he merited to be freed.

Besides also a great many wonders were obtained by his merits, which have hardly been handed down in the least particle of letters. But, commending these matters better to the almighty Lord, who alone does miracles, let us turn to the end of prayer.

Benediction

May your holy patronage, O Edward, most pious soldier of the eternal king, assist us, and coming down to our imperfection, obtain with your pious prayers in the presence of the most merciful judge that no insolence of human boasting would cast us down, that no impurity of lust would separate us from the most chaste embraces of the heavenly bridegroom, may no filth overtake our acts; rather, by your aid may we be lifted up to heavenly desires, so that we may merit to enjoy perpetual delights in the heavenly Jerusalem with all the saints, in the presence of our Lord Jesus Christ, who with both the eternal Father and the Holy Spirit, lives and reigns, God, through undying ages of ages. Amen.

Goscelin of Saint-Bertin (c. 1035-c. 1100) was a Benedictine monk and a prolific hagiographer of English saints, including St. Edward the Martyr's sister, St. Edith of Wilton. Born in France, he moved to England and was a resident of several monasteries.

Ryan Grant is a native of eastern Connecticut. He received his bachelor's degrees in philosophy and theology at Franciscan University of Steubenville. He taught Latin for eight years and has translated numerous works of St. Robert Bellarmine and St. Alphonsus Liguori. He resides in Post Falls, Idaho with his wife and six children.

Eric Sammons is the publisher of Saragossa Press and the author of several books, including *Holiness for Everyone: The Practical Spirituality of St. Josemaría Escrivá*. He holds a Master of Theology degree from Franciscan University of Steubenville. Through genealogical research, he determined that St. Edward the Martyr is his 28th-great uncle.

Made in the USA
Monee, IL
18 April 2022